The Lord's Prayer

Wycliffe Studies in Gospel, Church, and Culture

This series, emanating from Wycliffe College, Toronto, addresses key topics and issues in the church and in contemporary culture.

Grounded in the historic tradition of the Christian faith, the series presents topical subject matter in an accessible form and seeks to appeal to a broad audience.

The Lord's Prayer

EDITED BY
Karen Stiller

FOREWORD BY
Thomas Power

WIPF & STOCK · Eugene, Oregon

THE LORD'S PRAYER

Wycliffe Studies in Gospel, Church, and Culture

Copyright © 2017 Wipf and Stock Publishers. All rights reserved. Except for brief quotations in critical publications or reviews, no part of this book may be reproduced in any manner without prior written permission from the publisher. Write: Permissions, Wipf and Stock Publishers, 199 W. 8th Ave., Suite 3, Eugene, OR 97401.

Wipf & Stock
An Imprint of Wipf and Stock Publishers
199 W. 8th Ave., Suite 3
Eugene, OR 97401

www.wipfandstock.com

PAPERBACK ISBN: 978-1-5326-1658-7
HARDCOVER ISBN: 978-1-4982-4045-1
EBOOK ISBN: 978-1-4982-4044-4

Manufactured in the U.S.A.

Contents

Foreword | *vii*
  —Thomas Power

Preface | *ix*
  —Karen Stiller

1 "Lord, Teach Us to Pray" | 3
  —Terence Donaldson

2 "Pray Then Like This: Our Father, Who Art in Heaven" | 8
  —Judy Paulsen

3 "Hallowed Be Thy Name" | 12
  —J. Glen Taylor

4 "Thy Kingdom Come" | 18
  —David Kupp

5 "Thy Will Be Done" | 25
  —L. Ann Jervis

6 "On Earth as It Is in Heaven" | 30
  —Marion Taylor

Contents

7 "Give Us This Day Our Daily Bread" | 36
—Annette Brownlee

8 "Forgive Us Our Trespasses" | 40
—Alan Hayes

9 "As We Forgive Those Who Trespass Against Us" | 47
—Ephraim Radner

10 "Lead Us Not into Temptation" | 52
—Thomas Power

11 "Deliver Us from Evil" | 57
—Joseph Mangina

Bibliography | 63
List of Contributors | 65

Foreword

THOMAS POWER

THE SERIES ENTITLED WYCLIFFE College Studies in Gospel, Church, and Culture is intended to present topical subject matter in an accessible form and seeks to appeal to a broad audience. Typically, titles in the series derive from sermons given by the faculty of Wycliffe College, Toronto, in its Founders' Chapel. The current volume on the Lord's Prayer is the second in the series and derives from a sermon series given in the Spring of 2016.

I wish to thank my fellow contributors for their willingness to contribute to the current volume. I also want to express a special thanks to Rachel Lott of Wycliffe College for her work on formatting the manuscript.

Preface

KAREN STILLER

ONE OF THE EARLIEST memories I have of prayer, besides the "now I lay me down to sleep," slightly chilling bedtime plea, is of memorizing the Lord's Prayer. I wanted to recite it to my Sunday school teacher to gain another sticker on the memorization poster on our classroom wall. I didn't understand all the words back then, like "hallowed," and I thought daily bread was a literal request for those soft, processed white slices in the clear plastic bags that my mother kept in a bread box on our cluttered kitchen counter, perfect for quick sandwiches.

The Lord's Prayer—which is to be our prayer—is as familiar as those kinds of memories. Close our eyes and we recite it by heart. In some church traditions, we say the prayer together nearly every week, as a community standing before God. We call on those so familiar words and the comfort and direction they offer. The comfort that God is holy, that his kingdom is coming, that he provides just enough and that he can protect us from ourselves and from evil. The direction that we are to worship him, that we are part of this kingdom-coming work, that we have the discipline of forgiveness as almost a daily task, and that we are vulnerable to temptation, so being on guard is a fine idea.

The Wycliffe College faculty featured in this book take the Lord's Prayer line by line and excavate it for its forgotten meaning and its neglected treasure.

Evangelism professor Judy Paulsen writes, "Occasionally we must be reminded that the person in our parish whom we like the least, is the one we are praying alongside when we say 'Our Father,'" reminding us that the Lord's Prayer is set concretely in community.

In case our familiarity with the prayer has lulled us into thinking it is neat and tidy, David Kupp, professor of pastoral theology, writes: "The prayer is also dangerous, because when Jesus is teaching his community to pray to God 'your kingdom come' he is teaching them to pray for the end of the world as they know it."

The insights provided by Ephraim Radner, professor of historical theology, on that seemingly impossible call on us broken pilgrims to forgive, so that we can be forgiven, will bring you great relief if you are anything like me (at times, not so great at forgiving).

Each brief essay, pondering each line of this foundational prayer, guides us more deeply into the very things the Lord's Prayer requests: a sense of God's holiness, a sense of our own truest selves—broken and redeemed—and a glimpse of his kingdom, coming.

After this manner therefore pray ye:
Our Father which art in heaven,
Hallowed be thy name.
Thy kingdom come.
Thy will be done,
in earth as it is in heaven.
Give us this day our daily bread.
And forgive us our debts,
as we forgive our debtors.
And lead us not into temptation,
but deliver us from evil.

(MATT 6:9–13, KJV)

1

"Lord, Teach Us to Pray"

Terence Donaldson

The Lord's Prayer is not the only place in the Gospels where we encounter Jesus as a teacher of prayer. Jesus gives explicit teaching on prayer in several other passages. The Gospels record several other prayers of Jesus, along with more general references to Jesus as engaging in prayer, without any indication of the content of the prayer. So Jesus not only teaches his disciples about prayer, he models his teaching in his own prayer life.

But the Lord's Prayer is the capstone; here in a single passage, theologically rich and elegantly structured, we encounter Jesus both as teacher and as model. It is a wonderful prayer, providing us with a unique insight into the spiritual life of Jesus. Partly for this reason though, there are questions to be asked about how the prayer is to serve as a model for Christian prayer. That is, how might the prayer be seen as a response to our own request as Christians: "Lord, teach us to pray"?

This prayer differs from most Christian prayer—both elsewhere in the New Testament and throughout the history of the church—in that it is devoid of explicit christological content. The prayers with which Paul begins most of his letters, for example, are densely packed with references to Christ (e.g., six times in the little prayer at the start of 1 Cor 1:4–9). Often we end our prayers with the phrase "through Jesus Christ our Lord." By contrast, the Lord's Prayer is strikingly devoid of any references to the Lord, or to Jesus, or to Christ. It is a prayer that could be offered by any pious Jew in the first century.

Of course, someone may well object that the presence of the Lord in the Lord's Prayer is everywhere evident, even if implicitly. It is the prayer taught by the Lord Jesus, after all, in response to a request from his closest followers. When we recite it, we are repeating the words of Jesus himself. The objection is not without force, but the question remains and is not to be simply set aside: How can this prayer, which says nothing explicitly about the life, death, and resurrection of Jesus the Christ, serve as a model of prayer for the church—the community that has been called into being precisely by these events?

The objection points us in the direction of an answer. If the prayer has ongoing significance—if it is a prayer not simply for the disciples during the earthly ministry of Jesus, but also for the church—the significance is to be found in the fact that it is Jesus' own prayer. It is Jesus' own prayer not simply in that he taught it, but also in that it was his own prayer to the Father, a prayer rooted in his own earthly ministry.

The prayer is framed with first-person plurals: our Father, give us, forgive us, do not bring us, deliver us. Jesus himself joins with his disciples in this prayer. And Jesus invites his disciples to join him in his own prayer.

All the elements of the prayer relate in significant ways to aspects of Jesus' own ministry and mission. Remember, his willingness to depend on God for the provision of daily bread was one of the issues in the temptation, as was the readiness to worship God alone and thus to sanctify God's name. The petition for the coming of God's kingdom or rule leads us directly to the heart of Jesus' proclamation and teaching: "Repent, for the kingdom of God has drawn near." We also hear him say "The kingdom of God is like . . . " someone who sowed seed in a field, or mixed yeast with flour, or found a treasure in a field. The nature and coming of the kingdom was central for Jesus. We see echoes of his ministry and mission again in the petition to be spared the time of testing. Jesus was to pray this again in the Garden of Gethsemane, though there he also showed himself ready to undergo the trial in order that God's will might be done on earth. And even the petition to be forgiven our debts or trespasses is not without resonance. Jesus saw his whole life and his death as a redemptive self-offering, given as a ransom for many, for the forgiveness of their sins.

We are invited to see the Lord's Prayer not simply as a lesson taught by a teacher to his disciples, but as an invitation to enter into the life and mission of the teacher himself. The prayer is, in a very deep sense, Jesus' own prayer. It arises out of the core of his mission as messiah and son. And yet, by inviting his disciples to share in this prayer, he calls them into participation with him in the mission.

So we see the prayer is deeply christological and thus deeply Christian. As the prayer of Jesus himself, it is located squarely at the center of his mission as messiah and son. As a prayer that Jesus invites his disciples to share, it serves to signal our participation with Christ in this process of redemptive self-offering and cross bearing, of death to this age and rising to the life of the age to come. We catch a glimpse of the pattern of identification and participation that was profoundly summed up by Irenaeus in his well-known sentence: "Christ became what we are in order that we might become what he is."

On one hand, we have Christ's full identification with the human situation, his becoming what we are. In the first instance, this was a full identification with Israel. Remember, none of these petitions was startlingly new. Most of them find parallels in Jewish prayers of the day. Jesus' mission as messiah and son was deeply rooted in the life, faith, and hope of the faithful within Israel. But Jesus' full identification with Israel was, at the same time and in a particular way, identification with the whole of humankind. His mission was a continuation of—and a fulfillment of—the calling of Israel itself. Israel's election out of all the nations of the world was to result, eventually, in the blessing of all the nations of the earth, in the appearance of a light that would enlighten the Gentiles.

Identification, though, is just part of the story. Yes, Christ fully identifies with the human situation, even to the point of death, but it is more than that. Jesus remains faithful even to the point of death. He sanctifies God's name. He depends on God for sustenance. He subordinates his own will to that of the Father even at the cost of his own life. Jesus experiences fully the time of testing and trial. By living and dying in these ways, Christ defeats the power of sin and death, and throws open a way in which humankind might be delivered from evil and enter into the life of the kingdom of God—the domain where God's will is indeed done.

Jesus invites his disciples to walk in this cruciform way. It is this victory that he invites his disciples to share. In response to our question, "Lord, teach us to pray," Jesus does not simply respond with a stand-alone, independent set of petitions—even though those petitions are spiritually rich and nourishing. He invites us to participate with him in the process that leads from death to life. Identification, victory, participation: this is the christological pattern embedded deeply in the very substance of the prayer itself. May we immerse ourselves more deeply in the prayer and thus enter more fully into our participation in Christ.

2

"Pray Then Like This: Our Father, Who Art in Heaven"

Judy Paulsen

The disciples asked, "Lord, teach us to pray." And Jesus did. Perhaps this came as no great surprise from his closest followers. Jesus, after all, assumes his disciples *will* pray. He said "when," as he answers their question. He didn't say *if* you pray. If you have time. If you remember. If you feel like it. The act of adoring God, confessing our failings to him, thanking God, bringing our requests to God—these acts of prayer are to be as much of the Christian's life as breathing.

"*When* you pray, pray this way . . . " Jesus taught a prayer that is both a model for, and a teaching on, prayer itself. Implicit in the first words of the prayer, "Our Father, who art in heaven," is the idea that when we pray, we start with God. It may sound obvious, but this beginning is far from our natural bent. We so often begin with *our* questions, requests, complaints, or things for which we want to give thanks. Jesus says to start prayer with God. "Our Father in heaven."

Jesus intentionally uses the plural possessive *our* before Father. Literally, "Father of *us* . . . " Jesus seems to assume people will pray this prayer together, or at least pray to God while viewing themselves as part of a community.

We live in a fiercely individualistic culture. Our world is about what works for me. What's true for you. As Christians we've bought into this in multiple ways. We speak of a personal faith, a personal relationship, our own personal prayer life. These things are not wrong, but we must remember that when Jesus taught his followers *how to be* his followers, he always assumed they would be in community.

They would rub shoulders with each other—help each other, support each other, chastise each other, bother each other, encourage each other. Occasionally we must be reminded that the person in our parish whom we like the least is the one we are praying alongside when we say "Our Father." Some sibling squabbling is to be expected, but when we speak to God we not only speak as individuals, we talk to him together.

The word "our" bears not just a plural connotation, but also a *possessive* one. Jesus taught that we are welcome to use the word "our" to address the one living God, the creator of all that is or ever will be. We belong to God, and God to us. This is astonishing. It is beautiful. Jesus, the incarnate one, the Son of God himself, generously includes us in a relationship that is rightfully his alone. He said, "When you pray . . . pray like this . . . Our Father." These words, spoken by the Son of God to his followers, are a simple and profound demonstration of grace.

Now come the words "Who art in heaven," or in the simpler language of today, "Our Father *in heaven*." When teaching his first followers to pray, Jesus began by teaching about both the transcendence and the immanence of God.

God is the transcendent one to whom *heaven belongs*. He is all-knowing and all-powerful. He is the creator of all that was, and is, and shall be. He is the Holy One, worthy of our worship. So very different from us, dwelling eternally in perfect holiness—in the reality of heaven, where his perfect will is perfectly done.

And yet we can call him Father, a term that reflects God's immanence. The Hebrew word *Abba* means something close to "dad" or "daddy." It is a term of endearment and intimacy. If you listen closely while travelling in Israel today, you will hear little children address their fathers this way.

Sometimes in our churches there will be people for whom the word "father" has painful connotations. "Father" is not a term of endearment. They may have had a father who was absent or abusive, controlling, or maybe just too busy to bother with them.

The good news for those friends is not found in banning the word father, but in understanding that God wants to show us what the best sort of father is like: one who knows us deeply, provides for us, listens to us, disciplines, advises, and guides us. This father does all of this for the simple reason that he loves us. A good father knows our faults and failings and desires nothing more than to help us properly address them. A good father can see past the big mistakes we make and love us in spite of it. A good father will do everything in his power to help us thrive. We have the privilege of letting people know that their heavenly Father is indeed the best father.

Although he is the Lord of both earth and heaven, the Holy One, God loves us with the love of a father. Jesus reminded his disciples of wisdom from their own Scripture, as seen in this passage from Hosea: "When Israel was a child, I loved him, and out of Egypt I called my son. It was I who taught (my children) Ephraim to walk, taking them by the arms, but they did not realize it was I who healed them. I led them with cords of human kindness, with ties of love. I lifted the yoke from their neck and bent down to feed them" (Hosea 11:1, 3 & 4).

This Hosea passage is a beautiful description of the kind of love the very best father has for his children. This posture of being loved is how Jesus taught his first followers to start when they prayed. We pray with the knowledge of the transcendent God who loves us with the undying love of the very best father.

It is amazing that the Son of God would teach us to approach prayer with these words: "Our Father in heaven." May this phrase, in all its richness, gives us a hunger to spend more time every day listening to and talking with the One Living God.

The disciples went on, as we know, to heal, to preach, to teach, sometimes to die a martyr's death because of their love and devotion to Jesus—and because they had a deep understanding of their Father who is in heaven, and all that means.

3

"Hallowed Be Thy Name"

J. Glen Taylor

SOMETIMES THE SIMPLEST THINGS in life are also the most profound. This is certainly true of the Lord's Prayer and of the four words we are considering here: *hagiasthētō to onoma sou*. In context, here in Matthew's Gospel, Jesus' point includes: keep it simple.

And sometimes the things one mentions first are also the most important. This is also certainly true of these four words of Jesus' prayer. Indeed, in Luke, these *are* the first words of the Lord's Prayer, preceded only by "Father."

What makes these words both profound and important? It is not simply because Christians of all persuasions—Orthodox, Roman Catholic, Protestant—recite them regularly in their worship services. Nor is it only because the Lord's Prayer is central—literally and thematically—to the most famous sermon of all time, the Sermon on the Mount. It is because *without these four words, including their meaning and significance, life itself might ultimately be meaningless.*

The 2014 movie "Calvary" tells a dark tale about a Roman Catholic priest who is driven to despair by the doubts and cynicism of his townspeople. At one point a rich man bares his soul to the priest, played by Brendan Gleeson.

"I'm in a bad way Father. No, I'm not putting you on," he says. "Truth is, I've been in a bad way for a long time. Not wanting to do anything. Feeling of nothing being worthwhile. A sense of 'disassociation.' Detachment. I had a wife and kids. They meant nothing to me. I have money. It means nothing to me. I have life. It means nothing to me."

The priest, seemingly unsure of how to respond, asks: "Where do you think it comes from, this sense of detachment?"

The answer comes: "From nowhere. From nowhere."

A reviewer rightly commends the movie for its honest portrayal of the human condition, adding his own telling comments: "How many people in our own surroundings . . . are that honest with their own tribulations . . . pretending that everything is okay and talking about nothing? Fluff. Life isn't fluffy, it's downright hard. Emotions/traumas are having to be buried, down deep inside so that the pressure gets too much, and the path remains dark, or becomes explosive."

Unlike the people in this movie, some do find meaning in life apart from God. However, belief in God makes the job a whole lot easier. And it is a too-little known fact that such belief remains intellectually credible today.

Jesus was up front and unashamed to affirm that God exists. And what's more—and crucial—is that Jesus affirms that God is worthy of our respect. As one expert puts it, Jesus in this petition "asks God in the most reverent possible way, 'Please make your real identity known so that we and others will recognize and honor you as you really are.'"[1]

---

1. Bruner, *The Christbook*, 299.

A bit of history on the word "hallowed." The word draws from an Old Testament word *kavod*, which literally meant "heavy." The word has the same sense as the hippie term from the sixties, meaning "profound," even "cool." A theological dictionary takes the meaning back to the word "holiness," saying it refers in our passage to "God's innermost nature. It embraces omnipotence, eternity, and glory and evokes awe."[2]

One question remains about the wording of our petition: why hallow a person's name and not the person? Jews in Jesus' time (including many today) didn't utter the actual name of God but literally said "the name" instead—out of respect. As well, "the name" reminds us that we can never aptly describe God, because God is more than we humans are capable of understanding about him. (Even today many Jews will not type the word "God," typing "G-d" instead.) Further, "thy name" includes certain aspects associated with God, such as God's "reputation."

So why is Jesus' four-word expression so life-changing? Because it brings us to the heart of what Jesus viewed as bringing meaning to life itself: God. Not God as you or I might think him (or her) to be, but as God *really* is.

Another bit of background is helpful, in addition to the words "hallowed" and "name." Jesus' words are consistent with a secret to finding meaning in life that is contained in the Old Testament. The Book of Proverbs says: "The fear of the Lord is the beginning of wisdom." In other words, the place to start in order to find meaning and purpose in life involves, first, that God exists; and second, that God is substantive ("heavy") in terms of his power, character, being, and so on.

---

2. "*Hágios* in the NT," 16.

J. Glen Taylor: *"Hallowed Be Thy Name"*

But Jesus is claiming more than a truth from the Old Testament wisdom tradition. Remember, in the Old Testament God is so "heavy" as to belong to a category all of his own. God is normally understood to be beyond our ability fully to understand, as indeed he is. But we must also remember who it is that is teaching us to pray this prayer: Jesus. Not some mere human, but also *God* incarnate, Jesus here reflects his own (full, divine) intimate knowledge of God. The term "Father" reflects this extraordinary knowledge of the Hallowed One. What's more, by saying "'our' Father," Jesus invites *us* to join his own intimate, eternal relationship of knowing God!

By teaching us to pray "Hallowed be Thy name," Jesus does not give us a lesson on freedom from despair in life, at least directly. He is telling us what to pray. Yet Jesus' overwhelming preoccupation with the honor and glory of God—essentially the inherently flattering triumphant agenda of God, encapsulated in the words "thy kingdom come" which come next in the prayer—summons us away from ourselves and onto what really matters. And what is that? It is the plan of God, of which Jesus takes part, to manifest the fullness of his plan whereby creation will be renewed, his people redeemed, and his kingdom established.

I can think of no more pervasive error in our culture and in the church than our focus on ourselves, and each other—including all those truly worthy preoccupations with human justice, dignity, poverty, and so on—yet without the prior, more important, passion for the glory, holiness, and honor of *God*. Jesus put it well when he said earlier in this same sermon of which this prayer lesson is a part: *Seek ye first the kingdom of God*, and all these things shall be added unto you. Jesus' words have the effect of indicting us for our shameless "me-first," "if-it-feels-good-do-it" mentality.

We face futility and despair when we fail to recognize, or simply forget, that God and his concerns must come prior to, and underlie, all we do for the benefit of others, including ourselves. The commentator Bruner put it well in stating:

> The great need of the world is to know the primal weightiness of God and so become more weighty and significant itself. For without reference to its depth, the world is lightweight. The world's major need, and the First Petition reminds us of this, is to know God as God.[3]

In the movie "Calvary," after the rich man unburdens his sense of futility and despair, the priest responds by saying, "Look, I have to meet someone now. I'll call up to the house after. We'll talk. Get you back on track, OK?"

To which the rich man says, with hopeful sincerity, "thank you."

From this point on the fate of the priest tracks much the same way as that of Jesus. The priest never makes it to the rich man's house to patch things up. Instead, he goes to his meeting where, as the priest knew would likely happen, he is killed by a crazed man seeking vengeance for his childhood abuse at the hands of other priests who are long dead. The priest, in effect, dies for the sins of others.

With the prospect of his own vicarious death looming over him, the priest ends his conversation with the rich man by putting his hand on his shoulder and saying, with extraordinary concern, "You alright?", to which the man says, "Yeah." Again the priest asks, "Alright?" The man: "Yeah."

---

3. Bruner, *Matthew*, 298.

J. Glen Taylor: *"Hallowed Be Thy Name"*

There is in this exchange a faint bit of hope that is accentuated by another in the movie where the priest talks to his daughter. (He became a priest after becoming a widower.)

She says, "What is your greatest virtue?"

He replies, "Forgiveness. I think forgiveness has been highly underrated."

She says: "I forgive you . . . Do you forgive me?"

To which the priest responds: "*Always*."

"Calvary" the movie ends with the priest's daughter visiting her father's killer in prison. She picks up the phone behind the glass screen to speak to him. But the names of the cast roll before her words are uttered, leaving us only to guess that the daughter would forgive the man, if only to honor her father's commitment to the "always" of forgiveness.

The four words of the Lord's Prayer, "Hallowed be thy name," take a similar turn. God's character as magnificent and merciful *is* made known to us humans through Jesus' own death, a death he died for the sins of others, including ourselves. And the prayer, like the movie, concludes with a strong admonition to us to forgive others.

So, what shall we do? Forgive? "Always," says Jesus after this prayer is over.

But above all we should heed the summons of our Lord Jesus to pray: "May your name be hallowed." And in so doing our Lord shall be hallowed, his kingdom furthered. And somewhere along the way, too, our priorities shall be directed aright.

4

"Thy Kingdom Come"

David Kupp

If there are two words near the top of the list of most-decoded terms in biblical lexicography, they probably are "covenant" in the Jewish Scriptures, and "kingdom" in the Christian Scriptures. The mountain of commentary on each is nearly impossible to scale.

Does this mountain of commentary help us? When Jesus instructs us to pray, "Your kingdom come," what did he intend? What did his first generation of followers understand? What are we actually praying today when we utter, "Your kingdom come"?

Both ancient and modern peoples are wary of kingdoms and their various exercises of power, and often long for something better.

The many pathways to understanding "kingdom" remind me of a time in Kenya when a local community development team was going house to house in a cluster of villages in the district of Voi. They were conducting a baseline survey for a health and enterprise program. This team of Kenyans thought the task would be straightforward: go in, get the data, analyze it, report. Done. The government wanted a baseline of how rich and poor the people were.

David Kupp: *"Thy Kingdom Come"*

Then they would be able to ask us in three years: how well did you use our money? Did these projects increase the household incomes in Voi?

The team quickly discovered that in the local culture (as in other cultures), when you walk up to someone and ask, "How much money do you make?"—it doesn't go so well. It's a very personal question, often posed by your government, a kingdom. In most cultures, people tell an untruth more often in response to a question about their income than almost any other question. If you ask your neighbor about her monthly take-home pay, you'll soon discover the same issue. In Kenya, it was the villagers who helped us solve the problem by suggesting we look at "proxy indicators," rather than direct questions. The villagers taught us how to do wealth ranking indirectly, by comparing the number of steel and thatch roofs on houses, the range of latrine designs, types of cooking fuel, and numbers of motorcycle drivers.

Here's the link to the Lord's Prayer: Asking people how they like the local "kingdom" is about as awkward as asking about their income. Imagine yourself as a village development worker, conducting a survey in northern Palestine in the first century. You might ask, "Can you tell me on a scale of one to ten, one being low, ten being high, how you would rank the performance of the Roman emperor here in the Palestine in the past year?" It's difficult to imagine an honest answer being given. Yes, we are wary of kingdoms, in part because of what they may have done to us and our ancestors, and in part because of their character as empires. Empires are built by and for emperors: they tend to expand, they take over, they become oppressive. People suffer.

The Lord's Prayer

This petition in the Lord's Prayer, as Jesus gives it to us, is a dangerous petition. We are on very solid synoptic gospel ground here, historically and redactively. The kingdom of God, or the kingdom of heaven (as Matthew often calls it), is the central theme in the praxis and teaching of Jesus. It was not a device invented by the gospel redactors to give Jesus a coherent public relations voice. As Kraybill notes, Kingdom of God is genuinely Jesus' voice; it permeates all of his words, deeds and signs with notable clarity.[1]

Many residents in first-century Palestine were sick and tired of their Roman rulers, of the Herodians. They were weary of a long line of foreign kings and overlords, kingdoms, and empires. So they were excited about Jesus' continual references to the Kingdom of God. They longed for its coming. They were eager to pray for it and to find in it real change, even revolution.

The prophets (Ezekiel, Zechariah, Malachi, Isaiah) had talked about YHWH coming as king—YHWH would defeat the evil empire, free the people, create a new Exodus, return them to Zion. So here is Jesus apparently with the same battle cry: "Your kingdom come!"

So why is this dangerous? Because virtually no one understands Jesus' version of the kingdom. The misinterpretations are a solid gospel theme: hardly anyone gets the Kingdom right. A whole cast of characters misconstrue it:

- His closest followers
- The crowds
- The Jewish leaders
- The Roman rulers

---

1. Kraybill, *The Upside-Down Kingdom*, 19.

Herod, who perceives the infant Jesus to be a competing "king of the Jews," does not fathom the nature of this kingdom, and thus follows the slaughter of the innocents.

An exasperated Jesus finally shouts at his right-hand man: "Get behind me, Satan!" Jesus did not represent for almost anyone in his Palestinian world the sort of Messiah, and the sort of kingdom, they expected and wanted. And that's what got him killed.

It is notable that Jesus says: "Pray then in this way: Our Father in heaven . . . *your* kingdom come." Not Jesus' personal fiefdom. Not the disciples', not your, not my, envisioned kingdom. The Scriptures, the Gospels, our communities and churches, are full of kingdom makers, kingdom builders, kingdom pretenders. Jesus—in Matthew and Luke—sweeps all the pretenders aside, including his own disciples who were always jockeying for position. "Let *God's* kingdom come!" he insists.

The prayer is also dangerous, because when Jesus is teaching his community to pray to God "your kingdom come," he is teaching them to pray for the end of the world as they know it.

As F. Dale Bruner notes in his *Matthew,* Jesus is telling his disciples not to pray merely for changes in history. They are praying for a complete end to history and for the new world of God. A century ago Germans like J. Weiss, W. Wrede, and A Schweitzer helped New Testament scholarship rediscover Jesus' world of eschatology. We know now that the New Testament is essentially misconceived when not read through the sharp anticipation of the very near and impending transformation of life, the planet, the cosmos. Perhaps even as early as Jesus' entry to Jerusalem.

> "'Maran-atha' ('Come, Lord!') is the spirit with which almost every sentence in the NT was

> written and the spirit in which it is best read ever since. Indeed, the whole Lord's Prayer . . . is 'an extended Maranatha,' one great prayer for God's *final* coming."[2]

This is a dangerous prayer. It is a dangerous teaching by Jesus, a call for divine liberation and transformation of God's people, of their soil, their vineyards, their lands, their livelihoods, their communities, their world.

Equal, then, to how dangerous this prayer is, would be the ambivalence and *Angst* to follow, when the first generations of Jesus' earliest followers begin to die natural deaths without the full arrival of this new kingdom. At Easter the petition seemed to be working for the early church, but then for nineteen centuries Jesus' followers have wondered and debated to what degree that Kingdom is coming or has arrived. Is it present and visible, or absent and disengaged? Is it spiritually resident in the hearts and lives of his followers, or tangibly and powerfully implicit in slow and gradual penetration of the earth and all creation? And so we adjust, and wonder, and despair, and debate, and hope. And still we pray, "Your kingdom come."

The petition is dangerous because it is neither merely spiritual, nor merely political and social. It is both. It is both heaven and earth, now synchronized. Jesus does not teach us to pray: "in my *heart* as it is in heaven."

All of these first three petitions (hallowed be your Name, your Kingdom come, your will be done) are wrapped into "on *earth* as it is in heaven." The scope of Jesus' ministry is nothing less than the whole earth, from the smallest, quietest place of personal piety to the farthest expansion of the cosmos. And so we talk about justice, building peace, and love. We also talk about corruption,

---

2. Bruner, *Matthew*, 300; cf. Stendahl, "Matthew," 769–98.

the marred identities of the poor and the God-complexes of the non-poor. But note: this petition does not seek space for *you and me* to try forcibly to drag God's kingdom into place. No, we are to petition "Let Your Kingdom Come!"

Finally, when we do get it, it emerges that Jesus' version of the Kingdom of God is the Un-Kingdom, or the Upside-down Kingdom. If we are honest, we never do finish sorting out the difference between our highest aspirations for the Kingdom, and our ego-Empire interests in many forms, personal and corporate.

This is a present and unending wrestling match.

Some time ago, Donald Kraybill rescued some of my kingdom confusion, by helping me biblically to invert its meaning to the opposite of empire, with the gem he wrote nearly forty years ago, *The Upside-Down Kingdom*. The durability of Kraybill's thesis on kingdom inversion has seen it through six languages and now a fifth English edition in 2011. Kraybill reminds us that in Matthew the Lord's Prayer sits surrounded by the Sermon on the Mount. We know it is no accident that Matthew's Jesus looks like Moses here: Jesus ascends a mountain, and he delivers the ground rules of his new community in five sermons. Jesus delivers texts of transformation, texts of radical discipleship, and texts that later spell trouble for advocates of church empire. Jesus delivers here in the Sermon on the Mount a new form of governance, accountability, and community life, characterized by the particular behaviors of the Jesus community:

- They are humble, suffering, hungry for justice, and pure-in-heart peacemakers.
- They are a Jesus people, salty saints who glow in the dark, and intimate with the heart and pulse of the law and prophets.

- They are shocked by the fires of lust.
- They are careful about the impact of divorce on women within patriarchal systems.
- They are non-retaliating, enemy-loving, generous, and anonymous givers who pray in secret.
- They are happy, secretive fasters. Their lives, closets, basements, garages, and storage units are not full of stuff.
- They are clear-eyed, focused citizens of God's version of full life. Yes, citizens—not twenty-first century *consumers* racing down the treadmill of a carbon-choked life of casual air travel, disposable goods, and fresh mangos in winter.
- And they dwell in a kingdom where the manifold and repeated waves of anxiety beating on the shores of our lives—stop. And our fears about our clothes and food and drink and careers and reputations and browser histories and pathologies and being stripped naked in the public space, are replaced by the warm, calm contemplation of the lily in the field.

When we pray "Your kingdom come," are we truly begging for an altered cosmology? And with what content do we fill that? Is this a physical, geographic, spiritual, social, political, economic kingdom that fills the entire known universe with the principles and practices of God's reign? There is no greater challenge than to discover that pearl, and to throw everything we have at gaining it.

5

"Thy Will Be Done"

L. Ann Jervis

The phrase "Thy will be done" is the third of what are often called the heavenly petitions: "hallowed be thy name" is the first, and "thy kingdom come" is the second petition.

The third petition is found only in Matthew's version of the Lord's Prayer. Luke, the only other New Testament writer who gives us this prayer, moves from "thy kingdom come" directly to "give us today our daily bread."

Each of the first three petitions in Matthew is in the imperative mood (of course, Luke's first two petitions are as well). In fact almost all of the verbs in this prayer, whether in Matthew or Luke—in both parts of the prayer—are in the imperative mood. These verbs express commands.

In the last four petitions—the earthly petitions—the commands are in the active voice. Jesus is praying and teaching his disciples to pray that God would do something, such as God give us our daily bread, God forgive us our sins, etc. But in the first three petitions, the commands are in the passive voice—Jesus is teaching his disciples to pray that something would be done, that God's name would be hallowed; that God's kingdom would come; and that God's will would be done. The agent who is commanded to do this action is clearly our Father who is in heaven.

This is a puzzling way to pray. It is curious enough that Jesus directs us to pray in the mood of command, but it is even more curious that the first three petitions are in the mood of command *and* the passive voice. As if Jesus is teaching us that when we pray we are to direct God to get some things done: the hallowing of his name, the arrival of his kingdom, and the doing of his will.

There are a couple of aspects of this that make me squirm.

Does this mean that *God* needs our encouragement to be sure that God's own name is holy, to be sure that his kingdom comes, to be sure that his will is done? My understanding of God's omnipotence is challenged. It is as if God somehow needs us in order to be who God is. For surely God, being God, is one whose name is holy, whether or not I, or we, are involved; and God, being God, is surely one who does reign and whose sovereign rule will inevitably be manifest completely. He does not need us to make that the case; and God being God will necessarily have God's way. God's will *will* be done. Whether or not we pray for it.

What is this about, then? Jesus telling us to pray that God would make these things happen. What place do *we* have to do that? God is God and we are not. What a strange way to pray.

Not only does Jesus direct us to pray that God would get these things done, but Jesus teaches us to command God that God would get things done. Again, all of these verbs are in the imperative. My idea of how I should honor God is challenged. Surely I should come to God as a humble petitioner, eyes lowered, my head down, and pray to

God in the most deferential of ways. But, no, Jesus tells us to pray in the imperative mood.

Praying the prayer that Jesus taught is not simply to do what Jesus said, but to pray in Christ. We are praying as Christ, in Christ and through Christ, when we pray this prayer. This is the prayer that Jesus himself prays.

We might understand the first three petitions as how Jesus prays in his life with God in heaven, and the four earthly petitions as what and how Jesus prays as a human being who identifies fully with us.

This helps me make some sense of the strange form of the prayer. I can understand how Jesus, God's Son, might pray to God in the imperative. This is a sign of Jesus' absolute trust and complete faith in God. It shows us Jesus' deep intimacy with his Father.

Jesus is on such close terms with our Father who is in heaven that he can speak in the most direct of ways to him, looking God straight in the face, as it were. And Jesus does this because he knows that what he wants, and what God wants, are one and the same. If we understand that when we pray this prayer we do so as people who, as Paul writes in Galatians, are those who through our faith in Christ are now, along with Christ, children of God—then I grow more comfortable with the prayer.

Thinking of this prayer as participating in Christ's own prayer also makes sense of the strange use of the passive voice in the first three petitions. It is not that God needs encouragement to make these things happen—making his name holy, bringing in his kingdom, and having his will be done; but it is that God offers us access to the place that Christ has in God's own life. We, brought into the life of Christ, like Christ, may participate in the fullness of God's life. This is what God—our gracious God of love—has invited us into. Paul puts it this way in Colossians: "in Christ the whole fullness of deity dwells bodily, and you have come to fullness of life in him" (2:9–10).

In Christ, God welcomes us into the divine life. As far as we can surmise, God does so not only out of mercy, but fundamentally out of a love that truly desires us to share his life with him. A love so intense and deep that God would not be God without us. God loves us as a parent loves a child.

At the beginning of our Lord's Prayer, Jesus teaches us to pray in the mood of command, and in a voice that tells God what we want God to do: we want God to be sure his name is holy, to be sure his kingdom comes, and to be sure his will is done. Jesus teaches us that this is what God wants from us. We might go so far as to say that this is what God wants from us in order to be the God that God is. The God of such immense love that God includes us in God's very life and shares his own life with us. God privileges us with the capacity to be human beings who live in the divine life, who may look directly at God because we are clothed with Christ. Our God enables us to act as his son Jesus Christ in God's world.

We all know what that looks like. It looks like working for justice, caring for the widow and the orphan, feeding the hungry, and being willing to suffer for the sake of righteousness. The other time that Jesus prays the words "thy will be done" is in the garden of Gethsemane.

I have wondered whether instead of calling the constituent parts of the Lord's Prayer petitions we might call them performances. In praying these commands, we are bringing them into being as if we ourselves are Christ—the one who, whether he is in heaven or on earth, is perfectly attuned to God.

Performance, thought of not as artifice but as performance theory thinks of it, is a bringing into being, the making actual by means of speech. When we perform words, that performance does not just effect the words being spoken. Performing the words creates the reality that the words signify.

When we pray "thy will be done," we do so in Christ. Performing these words—and all of the words of this prayer—is to participate with God in creating this reality, or perhaps in unveiling this reality.

"Thy will be done" are words that proclaim what is and what is certain. Speaking them places us at the heart of reality—at the heart of God. As we perform them, as we pray them, we are taking part in the greatest performance of all—the cosmic, corporate, and individual transformation that God is enacting. It is the drama that leads towards the "telos" of God's will—the liberation of creation from bondage to decay and humanity's conformity to Christ.

Our Father: Thy will be done.

6

"On Earth as It Is in Heaven"

Marion Taylor

The spiritual practice of mediating on Scripture is commended by the psalmist, who describes the person who delights in Scripture and meditates on it day and night as blessed, fruitful, and even prosperous (Ps 1:1–3). Here, we seek to meditate on the discrete parts of the Lord's Prayer. We so often pray this prayer, in particular, without pausing to contemplate the meaning of its individual parts. To understand the meaning of the particularly cryptic line, "On earth as it is in heaven," we need to examine it first within its immediate context, and then consider its fuller significance within the larger context of Scripture.

The phrase "on earth as it is in heaven" is not a stand-alone phrase in the Lord's Prayer. Rather, it belongs to the three petitions that precede it: hallowed be your name; your kingdom come; your will be done.

Reading each of these petitions together with "on earth as it is in heaven," the phrase that actually joins them together, illuminates the meaning of all of these words of Jesus. When we pray the first petition, "hallowed be your name . . . on earth as it is in heaven," we are asking that the name of our Father, which is hallowed in heaven, be hallowed on earth. When we pray the second petition, "Your kingdom come . . . on earth as it is in heaven," we are asking that our Father's kingdom, which is present in heaven, may be seen here on earth. And when we pray the third petition, "Your will be done on earth as it is in heaven," we are asking that our Father's will, which is evident in heaven, be worked out here on earth.[1]

The phrase "on earth as it is in heaven" is comprehensive, and as Brunner suggests, it is cosmic and girdles the globe.[2] As such, it corrects some popular misconceptions about the self-directed focus of prayer and the spiritual life. Indeed, the phrase "on earth as it is in heaven" corrects the tendency we have to center our prayers on our own needs, desires, and concerns and those of people we know and love. While bringing such concerns before the Lord is legitimate, Jesus' teaching in the Lord's Prayer pushes us both upward and outward. According to the fourth-century church father John Chrysostom, Jesus is teaching us here that in praying we are "to take upon [ourselves] the care of the whole world. For [Jesus] did not at all say 'thy will be done in me or in us'—but everywhere on the earth."[3]

So what does this mean for us that our focus in prayer—and I would argue by extension our worldview—should be both upward and outward? There are many Scripture texts that help put a face on what it means to have an upward and outward focus in prayer and in how we view the world. The book of Nehemiah provides a helpful theological commentary on what Jesus is teaching us about when he says: "Hallowed be your name. Your kingdom come. Your will be done, on earth as it is in heaven."

1. Bruner, *The Christbook*, 304.
2. Ibid.
3. Ibid.

In Nehemiah chapter 1, we learn that Nehemiah lived in Susa, which was one of the most important capital cities in the Persian Empire. It was where Mordecai and Esther lived and the city where the prophet Daniel was likely buried. The story takes place about 445 BCE. Some of the Jews living in exile had returned home to rebuild the temple, and others like Nehemiah had decided to continue to live in exile where many of them were doing quite well for themselves.

However, Nehemiah's life changed dramatically the day his brother Hanani and his company came to visit following a trip to Jerusalem (Neh 1:1–11). Nehemiah asked them how the Jews who had returned to Jerusalem from exile were doing. Hanani's answer deeply disturbed Nehemiah. Hanani reported more than the well-known news that the community was still weak and small because of the destruction of 587 BC under Nebuchadnezzar. Rather, the devastating news he reported suggests another more recent disaster involving Jerusalem's broken-down walls and burnt gates and the inability of the Jews to defend themselves.

So how does Nehemiah react to this news about his fellow Jews?

We might think that the rich and administratively talented Nehemiah might jump into action immediately in response to the very real needs he has heard. Instead Nehemiah turns heavenward—he weeps, mourns, fasts, and prays for days. Nehemiah "prays as someone who is himself committed to what he prays about and he prays urgently to get God to take the action that only God can take."[4]

---

4. Goldingay, *Ezra, Nehemiah, and Esther*, 82.

Nehemiah begins his prayer by confessing what he knows is true about God, and he goes on to ask for help: "O LORD God of heaven, the great and awesome God who keeps covenant and steadfast love with those who love him and keep his commandments" (Neh 1:5). Nehemiah asks God to listen to his words. He recognizes the interconnection between heaven and earth. He repents of his sins and the sins of his fellow Jews. Then he boldly acts, so that God's name will be hallowed and God's kingdom will be present and God's will be done on earth as in heaven.

Nehemiah recognizes that he has an important role to play to enact God's will. But it's not something he does on his own. Nehemiah asks God for success and mercy on the mission he's about to undertake. He asks very specifically for God to make the Persian king favorable to his bold request that he—cupbearer of the king—be permitted to leave Susa and go back to Jerusalem to help rebuild the city (Neh 2:5).

I encourage you to read the rest of Nehemiah to find out how his mission to help God's people in Jerusalem goes. It was not without huge challenges. Nehemiah and those who worked with him repairing the walls and gates had many enemies, including enemies who were fellow Jews. But the project moves ahead, and in Nehemiah chapter 6 we read that the walls of the city were finally repaired. The very people who were trying to stop the rebuilding project admitted their defeat, for the project of rebuilding the walls was completed. It is remarkable that the project's enemies did not attribute the success of the repair work to Nehemiah and all the families that had helped him but to God (Neh 6:16).

"When all our enemies heard about this [i.e. that the walls had been completed], all the surrounding nations were afraid and lost their self-confidence, because they realized that this work had been done with the help of our God" (Neh 6:16, NIV). The translation, "this work had been done with the help of our God," misses the whole point of the Hebrew text, which says that "they realized that this work had been done by God." This verse acknowledges that the hard, sweaty, backbreaking work done by men, women, and children whose day jobs were not in construction and wall building, was really done by God, "on earth as it is in heaven."

The Old Testament is full of stories like this one that illustrate so well the concept of "on earth as it is in heaven." In Nehemiah, we see how God in his mercy used Nehemiah to respond to the needs of God's hurting people. Nehemiah did so with prayer, confession, and hard work, and in the end those who opposed the project recognized it was God's work. It was God's will. It hallowed God's name, and it built God's kingdom on earth. It was a work of divine-human cooperation: "on earth as it is in heaven."

"On earth as it is in heaven" corrects our nearsightedness. It is the vision correction we need when we, like Nehemiah, are so involved in our everyday lives that we are not aware of the needs of others or even of God's presence in our lives. May God open our eyes to recognize God's presence not only in our lives and our work, but also in the lives of others near and far. They, like the Jews in Nehemiah's day, may need us to get involved in their lives in prayerful and very practical ways. The phrase "on earth as it is in heaven" reminds us that God is here. God is involved in the rebuilding of broken-down walls and broken lives. He is present in the renewal of creation and even in the hard work of doing our daily chores and sitting by the bedside of someone who is dying. So as we pray the Lord's Prayer and pray,

> hallowed be your name.
> Your kingdom come.
> Your will be done,
> on earth as it is in heaven

we can remember Nehemiah's enactment of these petitions as he opened up his mind, heart, and hands to the needs of others. Together, with the rest of God's people, he worked to complete Jerusalem's walls, a project that provided security for the beleaguered Jews living there—a project God owned as his own. So too, let us live and pray with our minds and hearts and hands embracing both earth and heaven.

7

"Give Us This Day Our Daily Bread"

Annette Brownlee

Years ago, the American poet Sylvia Plath decided to stop washing her hair. The reason? She would only have to do it again. Now, Plath, whose poetry runs to the dark side of life, was known to have fragile mental health. So when she made this announcement it was not a good sign. But still, it is tempting to see her declaration not as a sign of slippage, but as an act of civil disobedience against the dailiness of life. Have you thought of what an accomplishment it is that somehow we get dinner on the table every night—every single night, somehow? We wash the dinner dishes, wake up, and somehow do it all again? And again.

My husband Ephraim and I went to visit his father and stepmother in their Quaker retirement community outside of Philadelphia. Rather than eat in their apartment they took us to the community dining room, which, since they began to allow residents to bring their own bottles of wine to the table, does quite a business. A couple at the table with us told us they eat there seven nights a week—it ain't cheap. Every single night, I asked the couple: "Don't you miss cooking?" The woman looked at me as a person not to be messed with and said, "I figured that in the first forty years of marriage I got dinner on the table about 12,000 times. I am done!"

In the prayer Jesus taught his disciples to pray, the "give us this day our daily bread" petition seems to mark a shift in what and how Jesus teaches his disciples to pray.

> Our Father, who art in heaven, hallowed be thy name.
> Thy kingdom come
> Thy will be done
> On earth as it is in heaven.
> Give us this day our daily bread.

Here Jesus seems to get more practical, teaching us to pray for daily bread. Is this the "earth" part of *on earth as it is in heaven*? Well, yes. Another poet asks, what are days for? His answer: Days are where we live. They are, as long as we are on earth; and the gift of days is what makes it possible for us to pray at all and to pray this prayer. "Seven times a day do I praise you because of your righteous judgements," the Psalmist says, and we with the Psalmist (Ps 119:64).

But we are not meant to leave behind how Jesus teaches us to pray up to this point. To have a sense of the connection between these two parts of the Lord's Prayer, it is helpful to remember *whom* he teaches to pray for daily bread. Whom? The ones who have just prayed that the Father's holiness be formed in them. The ones who have just prayed that the Father's will becomes their will. And so Jesus teaches us who have prayed that God's holiness and will be formed in us, to pray for *nothing* but our daily bread. He teaches us to pray for *no more* than daily bread. Not bread for the week, or month, or year; not bread just for me or my family or my tribe or nation. Give *us* this day our *daily* bread.

Why these two limitations? Because of whom he is teaching to pray. This is the place where holiness takes root, the soil in which our wills and desires are transformed—day by day—into God's.

What are the conditions that could possibly lead us to be able to pray for *only* daily bread and not a week's or lifetime's? (Isn't that what we want for our loved ones? A year or season or lifetime of safety and wellbeing?) What are the conditions that lead us to be able to pray not for my bread, or their bread, but only for our bread? The answer to both questions is the same: we trust in God's providence steadily at work in the world and the Church through and in Jesus Christ. This is the only condition that enables us to pray this petition Jesus teaches.

It is only when we trust that we are a part of a community that has Jesus as its head and heart. The only condition on which we could possibly ask *only* for our daily bread, is the person of Jesus Christ. And to us who have prayed that we might be holy and desire the Father's will as our own, that is just what Jesus teaches. Jesus teaches us to call fools the ones who fill their own barns and build extra storerooms for tomorrow's needs, with no regard for the hungry.

Only because of Jesus Christ is it possible to ask only for our daily bread. And we can and do pray only for our daily bread because of him. This *is* his prayer as well. This is the Lord's Prayer, not ours. He prays for our daily bread. He needed to eat. Every day. He had a body, limited by physical need and the round of the days. Our bodies. Like Israel in the tents, Jesus had to trust God to provide food every day. The limitations within this petition are the limitations of his divine life joined to our humanity. And so he teaches us to join ourselves to him, in his need and reliance; and in him we are joined to one another. Jesus turns to his disciples when they look at the hungry crowds at the end of a long day of teaching and says to them, as he says to us, "You give them something to eat."

Of course the tradition has understood daily bread in two ways. In Deuteronomy the connection between daily bread and the word of God is made explicit. "He humbled you by letting you hunger, then by feeding you with manna, in order to make you understand that one does not live by bread alone, but by every word that comes from the mouth of the LORD" (Deut 8:3). We live by every word that comes from the mouth of the Lord within the same limitations Jesus sets for our prayer for daily bread. No more than daily, as if faith could be hoarded. This is a reason the services of Morning and Evening Prayer are called the daily offices. And they are never just for ourselves alone. This is the reason that daily prayer is common prayer.

Give us this day this our daily bread. For us who have prayed that God's holiness and will be formed in us: *nothing* more than daily. Nothing less than our bread.

8

"Forgive Us Our Trespasses"

Alan Hayes

"Forgive us our trespasses." In these four words Jesus is telling us, first, that we need forgiveness; it's not that some are righteous and some are not. And this petition follows another about giving us this day our daily bread. It seems as we pray this every day that we need forgiveness every day.

Jesus is telling us that we cannot forgive ourselves. If we could, we wouldn't need to pray for it. Jesus is telling us—what every Jew would already know—that God does have the power to forgive. And the outcome of this prayer isn't certain. The prayer for forgiveness is not framed as a thanksgiving to God for guaranteeing our forgiveness.

If forgiveness came automatically, we could continue in sin so that grace might abound, as Paul puts the matter.

I'd like to offer two paradigms of praying for forgiveness. One is highly experiential, where we experience the burden of sin and we also experience the grace of forgiveness. The other is more ambiguous and incremental; it's about a spiritual discipline of prayerful discernment.

Stephen Daedalus in James Joyce's *Portrait of the Artist as a Young Man* experiences a dramatic burden of guilt and sin, and experiences a dramatic catharsis of absolution. In one long episode, we find Stephen at a Jesuit school in Dublin. He is 16. He's morally out of control and he's weighed down with things he can't talk to anyone about. The school has a spiritual retreat, and Father Arnall gives one of the greatest sermons in literature. He pulls out all the stops to convict the young men of their sins. Arnall exhorts them, he frightens them, he assures them, and he appeals to their sense of gratitude to God.

It works; Arnall moves Stephen to own up to his wretchedness. Stephen overcomes his self-consciousness and his self-protectiveness and takes himself to the confessional. There, with tears and anguish, Stephen blurts out everything, which, by the way, is more than the priest was expecting from a 16-year-old. The priest pronounces absolution. Stephen goes to a corner of the church to pray, and "[Stephen's] prayers ascended to heaven from his purified heart like perfume streaming upwards from a heart of white rose . . . In spite of all he had done it. He had confessed and God had pardoned him. His soul was made fair and holy once more, holy and happy. It would be beautiful to die if God so willed . . . Till that moment he had not known how beautiful and peaceful life could be . . . It was true. It was not a dream from which he would wake. The past was past."[1]

Stephen experiences a sweet liberation from a dark burden. But was that really divine grace that Stephen experienced? Or was it a stress-related emotional catharsis? Adolescent hormones? Was it simply wishful thinking? We can begin to answer by seeing whether Stephen begins to lead a converted life. Spoiler alert: he does not. Experience can deceive. And that works both ways. We can think we

1. Joyce, *A Portrait of the Artist as a Young Man*, 197–198.

are experiencing a forgiveness that really doesn't come from God; or we can fail to sense a forgiveness that God has already given us.

Instead of relying on personal experience, we rely on the Scriptures. And a good summary of what the Scriptures say on this matter of forgiveness is given in the Anglican Book of Common Prayer: "Almighty God of his great mercy hath promised forgiveness of sins to all them that with hearty repentance and true faith turn unto him."

- But how do we know that our repentance is hearty enough, or that our faith is true enough?
- Are they ever?
- And doesn't that make it sound as if we earn our forgiveness, instead of receiving it as free grace?

The English Puritans are among the wise Christian thinkers who probed into the psychology of sin and the experience of forgiveness. They realized the terrible paradox that faces sinners. Put more starkly than the Puritans ever said it, here is the paradox: if we feel right with God, we probably aren't, and if we feel alienated from God, he's right with us. If we feel at peace with God and ourselves, it may be because we are just, quite bluntly, rather dense.

Perhaps we have not seen how needy we really are. Maybe our attention has been focused on some particular issue in our lives that is not as large as we think it is, while we've totally overlooked some much deeper issues. Like how self-involved we are. How hardened are our hearts. How self-righteous we are, how angry we are. How wounded we are. After all, the people with the cleanest conscience are those who have no conscience at all. Yet, when we are really distraught about the state of our soul, when our self worth is zero, when we have no excuses to make and can't even hold our head up (like the tax collector in Jesus' parable), that's just when God is wanting to anoint us with the balm of Gilead, to heal our sin-sick soul.

As one of the Puritans said, care not for hell, for the nearer we feel it, the further we are from it.

One paradigm of forgiveness is that we experience a huge burden of guilt and then we experience a huge sense of forgiveness. I'm pleased for anyone who has had that experience. It is not one I could ever have myself. The other way forward is to search ourselves and train ourselves to see our need for forgiveness. This is an incremental process. We break up the big things into little things that we can work on. We learn to see the shortcomings in us that aren't so obvious to us, though they may be obvious to others.

St. Ignatius of Loyola, in his Spiritual Exercises, suggested a daily exercise of self-examination that he called an examen. It begins with a prayer for the grace of being confused about ourselves. Addressed to ourselves, confusion and shame are gifts. This is also the approach found in St. Augustine's *Confessions.*

The greatest obstacle to this stark self-knowledge is our instinct for self-justification.

It is almost fifty years ago that I began my theological studies. One of the issues that came up in my first year was demythologization, which was connected with a German Lutheran New Testament scholar named Rudolf Bultmann. It was a challenge to faith, and one of my professors gave me some advice. He told me I would have a very different view of Bultmann if I read his sermons. That was a lesson in itself, about not judging people on the basis of partial knowledge.

What struck me in Bultmann's sermons was his continual reference to the story of the Pharisee and the tax collector in Luke 18:9–14. Two people are praying. The religious guy justifies himself, saying, "Thank you, God, that I'm not like that sinner over there." The tax collector throws himself on God's mercy. And Jesus says it was the tax collector, not the religious man, that went home justified. Something in those sermons made me feel as if I had come to an understanding of the heart of the gospel like never before. Over the past fifty years I've kept those six verses of the Gospel of Luke very close.

The religious person in the parable justifies himself—because that is our instinct. We want to survive. We want to protect ourselves. We want to protect our egos, our sense of autonomy, and our sense of self-worth. We want to protect our fallibility—and to do that, we justify ourselves. We tell ourselves we did not do anything wrong. Or that it's someone else's fault. Or that we were forced. Or that it's just the way we are, the way God made us. There's a silly Will Ferrell movie where the bad guy frames Will Ferrell for something the bad guy actually did. At the end of the movie they confront each other, and the bad guy says, well, I didn't have a choice; it was either you or I. Will Ferrell answers: That sounds like a choice!

Society depends on this instinct of self-justification. You do not want heart surgery from a doctor who tells you that he makes a lot of mistakes. Juries aren't going to be impressed by lawyers who say they make a lot of errors. We don't vote for political leaders who tell us that they are almost always wrong. We don't want clergy that we can't look up to as good examples.

When Jesus teaches to pray for forgiveness, he asks us to know ourselves as we really are. That means renouncing our instinct for self-justification and self-protection, and throwing ourselves on God's grace. For me, it means admitting that as I write this chapter, if I stand before you preaching, I am a hypocrite. When I lead a class, I'm a sophist. When I make a purchase, I'm collaborating with an unjust economic order. When I tell myself that I care for others, I still have myself at the center.

I have excuses for all those things, and the excuses support my resistance to change.

In 1984, a lawyer named Marty Stroud was the lead prosecutor in a murder case in Shreveport, Louisiana. He won a conviction from an all-white jury against a black man named Glenn Ford, who was sentenced to death. Ford spent thirty years in a small dark cell without heat in the winter and boiling hot in the summer. Then evidence came to light that he was innocent. He was released. Marty Stroud wrote a long piece for the newspaper, confessing that he had got Glenn Ford convicted by using junk science and ignoring exculpatory evidence. Here's how he summarized things at the end:

> In 1984, I was 33 years old. I was arrogant, judgmental, narcissistic and very full of myself. I was not as interested in justice as I was in winning.... After the death verdict in the Ford trial, I went out with others and celebrated with a few rounds of drinks. That's sick. How totally wrong was I.... I end with the hope that providence will have more mercy for me than I showed Glenn Ford. But, I am also sobered by the realization that I certainly am not deserving of it.[2]

In one paradigm of forgiveness, we are weighed down by guilt, and we experience forgiveness. That happens

2. Stroud, "Lead prosecutor apologizes."

sometimes, though it is not always easy to authenticate. In the other paradigm, we are as clueless to the fact that we have a problem as the Pharisee in Jesus' parable. But we pray about our confusion about ourselves, we renounce self-justification, and we try to see ourselves as God sees us.

And when we pray, "Forgive us our trespasses," we can keep in mind the poem "Of God we ask one favor," by Emily Dickinson, which begins:

> Of God we ask one favor,
> That we may be forgiven—
> For what, he is presumed to know—
> The Crime, from us, is hidden.[3]

---

3. Dickinson, *The Complete Poems*, 1603.

9

"As We Forgive Those Who Trespass Against Us"

Ephraim Radner

For ecclesiology and Christology, this request is the richest petition of the Lord's Prayer. Forgiveness takes us into the midst of the Church, for the simple reason that Christ is the forgiving God come in the flesh into the midst of Israel.

The petition is not about my individual forgiving, or about God's forgiving of me as an individual. It is certainly inclusive of this, but not fundamental. If that were the case—if it meant "forgive me Lord in the same measure as I forgive others"—it would be the most hopeless of the petitions of the Lord's Prayer. Hopeless, because I *do not* forgive others, and to the degree I do not, I consign myself before God to the truncated dispositions of my own often necessarily limited spirit.

I certainly know people who have forgiven others, in human terms. As a pastor I have watched spouses forgive each other's betrayals, or children forgive their parents. And I know my forgiveness too . . . of those who have betrayed me in sometimes very deep ways. But what does this very *human* forgiveness amount to? We can get along again. There is access to smiles, to working together, to restored and genuine *bonhomie*. So it seems, and I can attest to that. But in every case of human forgiveness I know, including my own, one thing is lacking. And that is trust. We can forgive, but we are fools if we ever trust again. I cannot ask God to forgive me "just as" I forgive others; otherwise, as the disciples say in another context, "who then can be saved?" (Matt 19:25).

God, of course, neither trusts nor mistrusts us. He gives himself to us according to his will and purpose. And that is why, in fact, he can forgive at all. "I will remember not their sins" (Jer 31:34). Here is a truth to ponder: only God can forget. The rest of us gnaw on the bone. Please Lord, do *not* forgive me just as I forgive others! Every time we say the Lord's Prayer, we are, I hope, asking that we be saved from ourselves in this respect.

It is important to remember this prayer is in the plural. Jesus is speaking his instructions to his disciples as a group. The prayer is phrased as a "we," not an "I." Forgive *us*, as *we* forgive *others*. There is ontological weight to this plurality of voice. Forgiveness—our forgiving—is not about one person forgiving another; it is about *persons*, of which we are members, engaged in the work of forgiveness.

And this is so for a simple reason: we forgive another, not simply as someone who is wronged, but as a *doer* of wrong ourselves. If I forgive a sinner, it is only *as* a sinner that I do so. The great Russian-French Orthodox Christian Anthony Bloom describes this well: to encounter my enemy for the purpose of forgiveness, I must be unmasked myself as sinner, as enemy also. Only then can my encounter become one of compassion. To forgive as a human being is to enter a realm that causes *both of us* to tremble before God. To forgive is to *confess*.

E. Radner: *"As We Forgive Those Who Trespass"*

Bloom tells the story of when he was a young man attending church. There was a priest there, so "fallen," as an alcoholic, that he was no longer permitted to celebrate the liturgy. He just stood in church with everyone else. Bloom says that he used to place himself in front of the priest during services, so that the older man would have someone to fall on when he passed out. But it happened that Bloom needed to go to confession before Easter, as it was done in the Russian Church, and the only priest available was this one. So, going to see him privately, Bloom began his confession, only to have the priest break down in tears. What followed was not so much a mutual confession, as a kind of opening to truthfulness of the deepest kind. In *that* kind of encounter, God's forgiveness could take place: sinner with sinner.

It is no accident that the forgiveness initiated by one person going to speak to another privately, but face to face, finds its unveiled ending in Matthew 18, in an entire congregation's engagement. And while Matthew 18 is often invoked in discussions of ecclesial *discipline*, it is really about what happens when forgiveness breaks out within the church as a whole. I remind you of the whole center of the great East African Revival of the 1930s and beyond: Christians came together to walk in the light with one another, as they put it, to seek to put right that which was wrong among them, one to another, one among many, many before each other. And only then were the sins of each stirred up into the light, taken and laid at the foot of the Cross of Jesus. Then the great hymn breaks out: "Tukutendereza Yesu / Yesu Omwana gw'endiga"—We praise you Jesus, Jesus Lamb of God! We have found forgiveness together at the foot of the Cross! That is a communally transforming confession.

Forgiveness is ecclesial, because it is a work of many. But it is a work of many because it is the fruit of the great power and love of God who is light itself, in the flesh of Christ Jesus. It is Christ Jesus' coming as the God-Man—as God carrying the nature of all men and women—that thrusts the light not only into the hearts of this or that individual, but into the hearts of the whole race. The Church, you see, is the outworking of the Incarnation *racially*, Jew and Greek, nation upon nation, Adam and his children. Because there is a Him, there is an us. It is a hopeless reading of "As we forgive those who trespass against us," if the word "as" is read to be "in the manner of." But if the "as" means "just so," as in "just in the process, in the midst of" our forgiving others, just so forgive us Father. Then, what the prayer means is: Come among us, Lord! Send your Son! Let His forgiveness be revealed in our midst, in our encounter of sinner with sinner, seeking the light! Just so. Here! Maranatha!

This is how the Church came into being: "Father, forgive them, for they know not what they do" (Luke 23:34). In this act from the Cross, the world is shed with light; "what was whispered in dark" is now "shouted from the rooftops" (Matt 10:26). Sinners, forgiven together! And there, gathered in the upper room, frightened, waiting, are the disciples—and what do you suppose they are doing? Accusing, regretting, weeping, blaming, going back over each act and word, not only their own but the others' . . . searching for forgiveness, surely, in the only drawn-out and mixed-up way they could. They did this, why? Because the light had shone; and "in your light we see light" (Ps 36:9); and now we can see in the light who we are and how we are forgiven.

For into their midst had come the One who finally came through the doors and said "Peace! Peace be with you!" (John 20:19)—the Forgiver among those now working forgiveness, somehow. "Father, forgive them!" is in fact a translation, in divine words, of "forgive us our trespasses, as we forgive those who trespass against us." They are the same, because here at the Cross is the conjunction of Him and Us. And so he says not only "Peace be with you" to the broken disciples working their forgiveness, but he also says, "as the Father has sent me, so I send you" (John 20:21).

"Forgive us our trespasses as we forgive those who trespass against us." To pray this prayer, then, is to pray to *be* the Church, but not the church in general; we are the Church of *Jesus Christ*. Only this church. Only the church where forgiveness breaks out the way a cry breaks out amidst the silence, the way a sigh breaks out amidst the anxious, the way a song breaks out amidst the weeping. The way "joy breaks out" amidst the mourning (Ps 30:5).

There are persons I *need* to forgive, and have not been able to. I need to forgive them, and desperately so. And it is true in this individual sense: unless you forgive the sins of others your Father will not forgive you (Matt 6:15). But what I want to tell you—even as you too face this challenge, this impossible and hopeless challenge—is that it is not for me or you to do alone. It is for us to do together. I will need your help, and you mine. Will you help me forgive? That is not a sentimental request, but goes to the heart of God. Make use of confession and absolution, privately and together, formally, informally, singing and praying, in a tense gathering or over meals. But let us make use of it as bound to Jesus, whose light is given us just there.

10

"Lead Us Not Into Temptation"

Thomas Power

Of all the phrases that make up the Lord's Prayer, "Lead us not into temptation" is the most difficult with which to come to terms. Acknowledging God the Father in heaven, saying his name is holy, wishing his kingdom to come, desiring his will to be done on earth as it is in heaven, seeking provision for our daily needs, asking forgiveness for our sins as we forgive others, seeking deliverance from evil—all of those phrases are acceptable.

But to specifically request God not to lead us into temptation suggests that, on occasion, the Lord *might* do so.

- How could God allow this?
- How could it be for our good?
- Why might we need to ask for it not to happen?

First, remember that Jesus himself was tempted. The devil offered attractive things: provision, power, and protection from death. Jesus is tested for a divine purpose, but he does not sin.

Because he remained loyal in temptation, Jesus is the model for all believers when we are tempted.

If Jesus had never been tempted, would we be able to trust him? We know that Jesus can be trusted because, like us, he has been tempted. So Hebrews assures us: "Because he himself suffered when he was tempted, he is able to help those who are being tempted" (Heb 2:18).

Second, temptation is not a sin.

Remember what James says: "each person is tempted when they are dragged away by their own evil desire and enticed. Then after desire has conceived, it gives birth to sin, and sin, when it is full-grown, gives birth to death" (James 1:13–15).

Desire, sin, and death are progressive stages. Temptation is the desire stage. It is not sin. When we ask, "Lead us not into temptation," we ask that we be protected from evil desires, knowing those desires can progress to sin and death. By itself, temptation is not sin.

Third, temptation, because it is testing, can sometimes be for our good.

Tests, after all, are part of the human experience.

- Who could imagine an educational system without examinations? We do not know how good or bad we are until we take an examination and find out.
- There must first be tests to know that a new type of car is roadworthy or a new medicine is safe.
- We often require people to be tested before they can be trusted. If you go to hospital to have surgery, you want to be sure that the doctors have passed their examinations so that you can trust them.

Temptation is a form of moral testing. Our honesty, integrity, and purity are tested regularly in all kinds of situations. Satan wants us to fail in these tests, but God only wants such testing for our good. These experiences have the potential to bring spiritual growth. And so, because we fear failing such tests, we plead: Lead us not into temptation.

Fourth: yes, temptation is part of the human condition, but that does not mean we are free from responsibility to resist it.

Paul assures in 1 Corinthians: "No temptation has seized you except what is common to man" (1 Cor 10:13).

Remember, a firm "No" and a resolve to resist is Jesus' response to the allurements held out to him by the devil.

This point is stated practically by C. S. Lewis in his classic *Mere Christianity*:

"No (person) knows how bad he is till he has tried very hard to be good. A silly idea is current that good people do not know what temptation means. This is an obvious lie. Only those who try to resist temptation know how strong it is. After all, you find out the strength of the German army by fighting against it, not by giving in. You find out the strength of a wind by trying to walk against it, not by lying down. A man who gives in to temptation after five minutes simply does not know what it would have been like an hour later. That is why bad people, in one sense, know very little about badness—they have lived a sheltered life by always giving in. We never find out the strength of the evil impulse inside us until we try to fight it: and Christ, because He was the only man who never yielded to temptation, is also the only man who knows to the full what temptation means—the only complete realist."[1]

We are created as responsible people. No matter what we feel in the moment, it is up to us to do what we know

---

1. Lewis, *Mere Christianity*, 142.

is right. Resisting temptation is, in large part, a matter of discipline (1 Pet 5:8–9).

So why exactly then do we need to pray this unusual petition?

- We are asking God that we not be led into testing to the extent that it might overwhelm us.
- We are asking God not to abandon us to evil. Yes, allow us to be exposed to it in order to strengthen our characters and souls, but not to the extent that such exposure would cause us to succumb, in our human weakness, to the next stages of sin and death.

So what has God given us to guard against temptation?

God's word. Remember how Jesus overcame the devil in the desert. He used the same three words each time he replied to Satan: "It is written." Jesus' way out of temptation was to quote the word of God. If we immerse ourselves in it and memorize it, we will rely on it in times of temptation.

Prayer. In his trial in the Garden of Gethsemane, when Jesus returned to find his disciples sleeping, he cautioned them to "Watch and pray so that you will not fall into temptation. The spirit is willing, but the body is weak" (Matt 26:41). Alertness in prayer is key.

An invitation to rely on God's strength and power. We cannot deny the power of prayer, but ultimately protection from temptation is not dependent on our efforts but is grounded in God, his power, and his grace. This is what Paul says to the Corinthians: "God is faithful; he will not let you be tempted beyond what you can bear. But when you are tempted, he will also provide a way out so that you can stand up under it" (1 Cor 10:13). And in Hebrews: "For we do not have a high priest who is unable to sympathize with our weaknesses, but we have one who has been tempted in every way, just as we are, yet was without sin. Let us then approach the throne of grace with confidence, so that we may receive mercy and find grace to help us in our time of need" (Heb 4:15–16).

The ability to take responsibility by resisting temptation with God's help. Again James is helpful: "Submit yourselves, then, to God. Resist the devil, and he will flee from you" (Jas 4:7). We trust God to help us overcome our temptations, but we too must play our part in practical, common-sense ways.

Jesus' temptation in the desert occurred right after his baptism. Our baptism means we too will be called into the wilderness of temptation for our testing.

To ask "Lead us not into temptation" is to recognize our human weakness and vulnerability, that in times of temptation we need to draw on God's strength through prayer and God's word. That plea also acknowledges our need to be challenged in order that we may grow spiritually.

11

"Deliver Us From Evil"

Joseph Mangina

"And lead us not into temptation, but deliver us from evil."

When we recite the Lord's Prayer in worship, we are used to concluding it with the doxology, "for thine is the kingdom and the power and the glory, forever and ever, Amen."

In the Protestant world that doxology has long since become part of the prayer itself. Catholics, too, now stick it on as a sort of coda when the prayer is spoken in the Mass. But in the best manuscripts of the New Testament, the Our Father ends at this point: simply, deliver us from evil.

Deliver us from evil! What shall we say to this? Isn't it a sort of a "down" note to end on? And is it possible the doxology was added precisely because this ending seemed too stark, too abrupt, too negative? But just as Jesus says we are to pray simply, in secret and without parading our piety before others, so we are to conclude our prayers with the simple, urgent appeal that we be delivered from evil in its many forms.

There are many reasons to pray to God: to praise him, to thank him, to bless him, to proclaim him in the midst of the congregation. But to the extent that human life always involves suffering, so our situation when we pray is never very far from the need for deliverance. Lead us not into temptation, but deliver us from evil!

In teaching us so to pray, the Lord truly stoops down to meet us where we are.

Kate Bowler is a talented church historian at Duke Divinity School who does research on the prosperity gospel. Kate is a remarkably sympathetic student of the movement. She doesn't condescend or criticize. She genuinely likes the people she studies—a wonderful trait in a historian or sociologist, and I might say, not a bad trait in a priest or pastor as they relate to their congregation. I heard Kate speak about the true believers in prosperity religion, and I couldn't help thinking they are missing something important about the real gospel, which is to say the gospel of Christ. Prosperity religion says that by thinking positively and believing hard enough, we can avoid illness, find a mate, and perhaps even make a little money into the bargain. Dear Lord, I would really, really like that Lamborghini, or if that may not be, at least a Porsche Carrera . . . Doesn't God want to bless his children? There is something very elemental and human about all of this. Prosperity believers seem hungry for affirmation and look for it in God's involvement in the smallest details of their lives, as evidenced in visible and material blessing. We should not be too quick to condemn.

But at the same time there is something deeply inhuman about it, insofar as it raises the false hope that being a Christian must generate abundance and emotional satisfaction, in a directly causal way. Faith => blessing. As Kate Bowler says, what she found all too often among prosperity gospel folk was a sense of exhaustion. It is exhausting to go through life expecting that you should—must!—be healthy, wealthy, and above all smiling. And what happens to faith when these blessings fail to materialize? Should we blame the victim, or should the victim blame herself? God forbid.

By contrast, the petition "deliver us from evil," like the Lord's Prayer as a whole, sets us firmly in the midst of a world where bad things happen to good people, and to bad people, and to all people. Jesus does not need to specify what the evils are. We know them well enough. He is happy to let us fill in the blanks. Life so often hurts—to be human is to be vulnerable, anxious, conflicted, confused—and so we have full liberty to bring our needs before God, and to ask him to rescue us from ills great and small.

In this sense, the conclusion to the Lord's Prayer fits with the tone of confidence, a child's confidence in its father or mother, that frames the prayer as a whole. Our Father in heaven . . . deliver us from evil. For your name's and your great goodness' sake, preserve us your children from all harm.

It is Matthew who gives us this petition. Luke omits it, or Matthew adds it. Take your pick. I will leave it to my colleagues in New Testament to work out the synoptic problem in this matter. The book of John, the fourth gospel, does not include the Lord's Prayer, nor does Jesus in this gospel ever teach his disciples to pray. Rather he prays for them—and at great length! John 17, the famous High Priestly Prayer, is Jesus' extended petition on behalf of the disciples for the time following his return to the Father. And in the midst of that prayer we read:

"I do not ask that you take them out of the world, but that you keep them from the evil one. They are not of the world, just as I am not of the world. Sanctify them in the truth; your word is truth. As you sent me into the world, so I have sent them into the world. And for their sake I consecrate myself, that they also may be sanctified in truth."

In this passage, John makes clear what Matthew only hints at, namely that what we need saving from is not just evil in some abstract, generic sense but "the evil one" (the Greek expression *tou ponerou* can be read either way). For John, it is obvious that the world is the domain of the devil. And because the disciples are being sent into the world—into enemy territory, as it were—they require special protection.

Christ's will for his followers is sanctification, holiness, and truth; and for the sake of that truth, he prays that they, which is to say we, may be protected from the evil one.

Jesus in both Matthew 6 and John 17 says exactly as much about the devil as we need to know, namely, that he is evil. We can so easily get caught up in speculations about the origins of the devil, his ontological status, the extent to which he is "personal," whether he is a fallen angel, and so on. Such questions may have their place in the theological classroom. But in the context of the Christian life, all we really need to know about the devil is that he is evil; that he is bad for us; that he wills our destruction, even as the Lord God wills our good. The devil as a cartoon character is a comical figure. The devil in literature is often romantic and debonair. The devil in real life is brutal, destructive, and ugly. He shows his face in human bombs going off in a Brussels airport; in the slow, demeaning process of spousal or child abuse; in the violent bad sex that's been so much in the news of late. Whatever else evil or the evil one may be, it is certainly not "cool."

Joseph Mangina: *"Deliver Us From Evil"*

In Matthew, "deliver us from the evil one" is the Church's prayer. In John, "keep them from the evil one" is Jesus' prayer for his Church. What is the Church? It is that community that, day by day, asks God to preserve it from evil—not just from suffering evil but from committing it. Today, this one day, we ask that we may not add to the world's quantity of horror. We will not speak harshly to our children. We will not play the power games of ecclesial or academic or civil politics. We will not suck up to the powerful, or ignore the claims of the weak and vulnerable. We will not shun people who seem just a bit odd—well, let's face it, who *are* odd—and who therefore threaten our sense of self. We will not do these things because we are Christians, and because, well, we simply cannot and will not. We will not do them because as God's sanctified ones we do not belong to "the world," as Christ Jesus does not belong to the world.

Well, who are we kidding? We, the Church, God's sanctified people, act a lot of the time as though we were anything but. The evil that defines the world is too often in our own hearts. And so if the Church is holy—and I believe the Church is holy—its holiness must come from a source outside itself. The Church must pray for its sanctity; it must long and yearn for it; and yes, it must also act on it—but act in such a way as to open its heart, our hearts, to the One who has promised to sanctify us in the truth.

And so we pray: Father in heaven, deliver us from evil! Has not the Father answered this prayer in advance? Did he not answer it, first, by handing Christ over to the power of evil for our sake? And then once and for all by raising him from the dead? To pray "deliver us from evil" is not so much to ask God to fix things for us, but to bring us into the presence of Christ, who is the embodied answer to all our prayers. In Christ the Church prays with confidence for deliverance, in the knowledge that God is the one who practices resurrection and ushers in the new creation—here, now, this day and always.

Bibliography

Bruner, Frederick Dale. *The Christbook: A Historical/Theological Commentary: Matthew 1–12.* Waco, TX: Word, 1987.

———. *Matthew: A Commentary.* Grand Rapids, MI: Eerdmans, 2007.

Dickinson, Emily. *The Complete Poems.* Edited by Thomas H. Johnson. New York: Little, Brown, & Co., 1961.

Goldingay, John. *Ezra, Nehemiah, and Esther for Everyone.* Louisville, KY: Westminster John Knox, 2012.

"*Hágios* in the NT." In *Theological Dictionary of the New Testament* (abridged), edited by Gerhard Kittel and Gerhard Friedrich, translated by George W. Bromiley, 16–17. Grand Rapids, MI: Eerdmans, 1985.

Joyce, James. *A Portrait of the Artist as a Young Man.* Modern Library. New York: Random, 1996.

Kraybill, Donald. *The Upside-Down Kingdom.* Scottdale, PA: Herald, 1978.

Lewis, C. S. *Mere Christianity.* New York: Harper-Collins, 2001.

Stendahl, Krister. "Matthew." In *Peake's Commentary on the Bible*, edited by M. Black and H. H. Rowley, 769–98. London: Routledge, 1962.

Stroud, A. M. "Marty" III. "Lead prosecutor apologizes for role in sending man to death row." *The Shreveport Times* (March 20, 2015). http://www.shreveporttimes.com/story/opinion/readers/2015/03/20/lead-prosecutor-offers-apology-in-the-case-of-exonerated-death-row-inmate-glenn-ford/25049063/.

List of Contributors

Annette Brownlee
Chaplain, Professor of Pastoral Theology and Director of Field Education

Terence Donaldson
Lord and Lady Coggan Professor of New Testament Studies

Alan L. Hayes
Bishops Frederick and Heber Wilkinson Professor of Church History

L. Ann Jervis
Professor of New Testament

David Kupp
Professor of Pastoral Theology

Joseph Mangina
Professor of Systematic Theology

Judy Paulsen
Professor of Evangelism, Director of the Institute of Evangelism

LIST OF CONTRIBUTORS

Thomas Power
Adjunct Professor of Church History, Theological Librarian

Ephraim Radner
Professor of Historical Theology

J. Glen Taylor
Professor of Scripture and Global Christianity

Marion Taylor
Professor of Old Testament

Karen Stiller is a senior editor of Faith Today magazine, freelance writer, and general editor of *Evangelicals Around the World: A global handbook for the 21st century* (Thomas Nelson, 2015) and co-author of *Shifting Stats Shaking the Church: 40 Canadian Churches Respond* and *Going Missional: Conversations with 13 Canadian Churches who have Embraced Missional Life*.

www.ingramcontent.com/pod-product-compliance
Lightning Source LLC
Chambersburg PA
CBHW070101100426
42743CB00012B/2625